LITTLE LIBRARY

A Visit to
France

Simon Buckland

Kingfisher Books

Contents

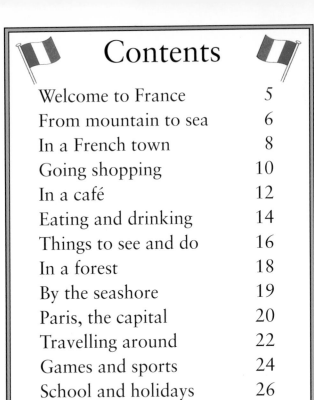

Welcome to France

L ate in the afternoon a taxi pulls up in a small French town and a family of tourists gets out. As they cross to their hotel, they see a woman carrying home two freshly baked *baguettes* – long crusty French loaves.

Delicious food is just one of the things you'll enjoy if you visit France. As you're about to discover, there are all sorts of other fun things to explore.

From mountain to sea

France is a very large country with lots of different landscapes. There are long sunny beaches in the south, while the northwestern coastline is rockier and dotted with fishing villages. To the east are snow-covered mountains – the Alps. Inland, there are orchards and vineyards, and along the peaceful valley of the Loire River, beautiful old *châteaux* (castles).

FRENCH MONEY

In France, the money people use is called francs and centimes (100 centimes = 1 franc). When you go to a bank, you'll see signs showing how much French money you can get in exchange for your own money.

United
Kingdom

Netherlands

Belgium

Germany

*English
Channel*

R. Seine

Paris

ATLANTIC
OCEAN

R. Loire

FRANCE

Lyon

ALPS

Bordeaux

R. Rhône

Toulouse •

• Marseille

Spain

MEDITERRANEAN
SEA

In a French town

Nearly all French towns and villages have a main square, with a variety of shops all around it. There's always a café where you can sit outside if the weather is good. Cafés are great places to meet friends and watch the world go by!

① Post office
② Chemist
③ Newsagent
④ Bank
⑤ Butcher

BREAD AND CAKES

France is famous for its crusty bread and delicious cakes. The *boulangerie* is for bread and the *pâtisserie* for cakes – but usually they are just one shop.

For breakfast, try the crescent-shaped rolls called *croissants* or a *pain au chocolat* (with chocolate inside).

⑤

MARCHE BOUCHERIE HOTEL Tabac

Café

In most places, there is a market at least once a week. Local farmers set up stalls and sell fresh fruit, vegetables, cheese and other produce. You might even see live chickens and rabbits for sale.

Going shopping

I f you want to buy some postcards to send home to friends, you'll find them in the *maison de la presse*, along with comics, newspapers, books, pens, sweets and even toys. Stamps are usually sold at a *tabac* (tobacconist's).

In most towns, shops are closed on Sundays and Mondays. In country areas they close every day at lunchtime, too.

△ Cheese is sold in an *épicerie* (grocery shop). The French like to eat lots of different cheeses at the end of a meal. Try a mild and creamy one, such as camembert.

timbres
stamps

carte postale
postcard

bonbons
sweets

stylos
pens

jouet
toy

In a café

Y ou can buy all sorts of drinks in a French café. You might like to try a delicious fresh lemon drink called *citron pressé*, or a *chocolat chaud* (hot chocolate). A café will serve tasty snacks at any time of the day, but you'll have to go to a proper restaurant if you want a full meal.

CROQUE-MONSIEUR

You'll find this sandwich on the menu in every café. A *croque-madame* has a fried egg on top.

1 Put a slice of cheese on a piece of bread, add a slice of ham, then more cheese, and finally a slice of bread.
2 Toast it under a grill until it's golden brown on both sides and the cheese has melted.

Ice-cream is called *glace*. There are lots of delicious flavours – try *fraise* (strawberry) or *framboise* (raspberry).

CITRON PRESSE

You'll need:
4 large lemons
8 tsp white sugar
2 litres cold water
Lots of ice

1 Ask a grown-up to help you cut the lemons in half and squeeze the juice out of them.
2 Pour the juice into a large jug and stir in the sugar.
3 Add the cold water and lots of ice. Drink it while it's still cold. *Santé* – cheers!

Eating and drinking

The French love eating out, and you'll often see whole families together at a restaurant, from very small children to grandparents.

Meals can have four courses and take as long as two hours to eat. Lunch is usually between 12 and 2 pm, while dinner is from 7.30 pm onwards.

A meal may start with soup, cold meats, *pâté*, or even snails cooked in garlic butter.

There may be seafood next. Then there's a meat course, such as chicken or steak.

As soon as you sit down, the waiter will bring you a basket of fresh bread. French people eat bread with most meals.

People drink wine with meals in France. Often children are allowed to drink it watered down.

The fourth course can be cheese or a dessert – sometimes you can have both!

Each area of France has its own special desserts, but you'll usually find a fruit tart on the menu.

Things to see and do

There are lots of interesting places to go to in France. Here are just a few of the sites tourists like to visit.

The Dordogne is a beautiful hilly and wooded region in southwestern France. It's a good place for walking and canoeing holidays. There are caves to explore, too!

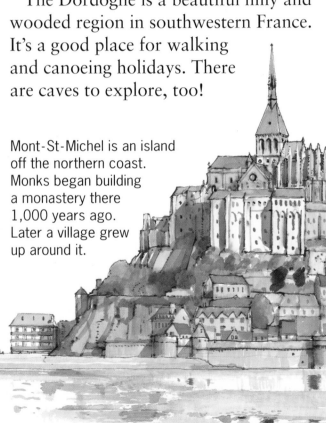

Mont-St-Michel is an island off the northern coast. Monks began building a monastery there 1,000 years ago. Later a village grew up around it.

△ Some of the caves in the Dordogne have paintings in them which were made more than 12,000 years ago. The most famous are at Lascaux.

Many towns have an aquarium, where you can see all sorts of exotic fish swimming about.

In a forest

There are large forests throughout France, with tracks to walk along. You may see French families collecting mushrooms in the autumn. They go to the chemist's to check which ones are safe to eat.

△ The *cèpe* has a nutty taste. It's called the edible boletus in English.

△ The *chanterelle* grows right next to trees. It's tasty, but very hard to find.

Many wild mushrooms are poisonous, so it's safest to let grown-ups pick and cook them.

By the seashore

I f you visit the seaside, try looking under rocks and in rockpools for some of the shell-fish shown below. You will find them on the menu in most French restaurants.

◁ You may find great bunches of mussels fixed to rocks. Take care, as their shells are very sharp.

▷ Prawns are often trapped in rockpools when the tide goes out. The greyish ones are more common than the larger, pinkish ones.

▷ You need to be lucky to find a lobster. It is fierce and blue when alive, but turns red when cooked.

Paris, the capital

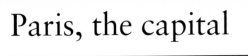

Many people think that Paris is the world's most beautiful city. It grew up along the banks of the river Seine 2,000 years ago. The oldest part is an island, the Ile de la cité.

▽ One of the best ways of seeing Paris is to take a river trip in a *bateau-mouche*.

△ You don't have to walk to the top of the Eiffel Tower to see over the whole city – there's a lift!

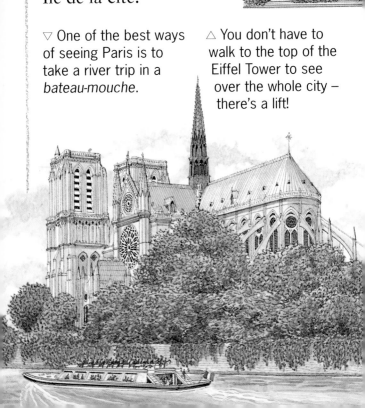

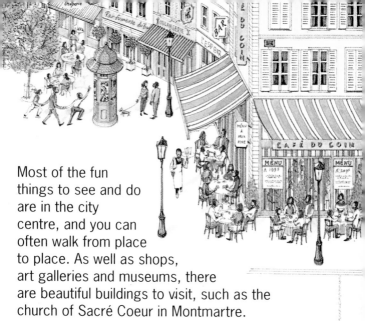

Most of the fun things to see and do are in the city centre, and you can often walk from place to place. As well as shops, art galleries and museums, there are beautiful buildings to visit, such as the church of Sacré Coeur in Montmartre.

GETTING ABOUT

If the place you want to visit is too far to reach on foot, then take a ride on a train. The underground railway is called the *métro* in Paris. The entrances to some of the older stations have superb ironwork decorations.

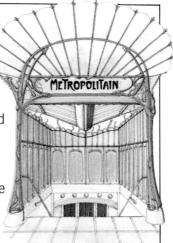

Travelling around

F rance is a big country, but easy to travel around. It has the fastest trains in the world – and some of the slowest boats! There are good roads and in country areas, little traffic.

△ The fastest way is on the TGV. This high-speed train looks like a rocket and shoots along at nearly 300 km/h.

▽ One of the slowest ways to travel is on a canal boat.

Bicycling is a peaceful way to explore the countryside. You can often hire bikes from railway stations.

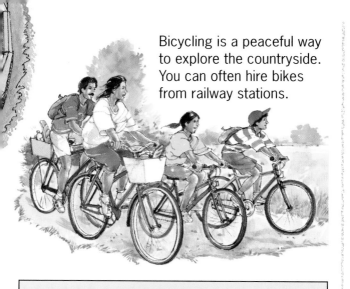

MOTORWAYS

French motorways are called *autoroutes*, and they link Paris to all of the main cities in the country. They aren't free – when you see the sign saying *péage* (toll), you have to stop and pay.

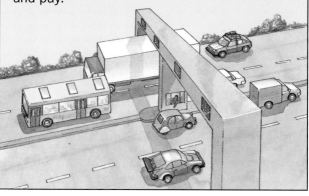

Games and sports

Wherever you go in France, you'll find groups of people playing *pétanque*. This game is something like bowls, but it uses metal balls that are thrown, not rolled.

One of France's major sporting event is the Le Mans car race. Drivers cover about 5,300 km in 24 hours.

PLAY A GAME OF PETANQUE

You'll need a couple of friends, a small ball and some larger, heavy ones – cricket balls would do. It's best to play on level ground.

The small ball is the *cochonnet* (little pig). Put it down and mark a throwing line about 5 metres away from it.

Standing at the throwing line, take turns with your friends to throw one of the heavy balls towards the *cochonnet*. The person whose ball is closest to it wins.

School and holidays

Children have to get up early, as some schools begin at 8.00 am. It's a long day, often going on until about 5.00 pm, but the lunch break lasts for about two hours. There are often Saturday morning classes, too, but Wednesday is usually a holiday.

Some children go home for lunch. Others eat in the canteen, and then play in the school yard.

Children are lucky because there are lots of special holidays and festivals in France. On 14th July the whole country honours Bastille Day. There are parties and fireworks to celebrate the start of the French Revolution in 1789.

MAKE A CROWN

On 6th January, people celebrate the *fête des rois* (festival of the three kings) by eating special cakes. There's a little bean or model in some cakes. Whoever finds it wears a crown and is king or queen for the day.

1 Measure around the top of your head and cut a piece of card 20 cm longer and 10 cm deep.
2 Cut triangles out of the top edge. Staple the ends together, then paint your crown gold.
3 Now ask a grown-up to bake some special cakes for you. Make sure one cake has a bean in it, so someone can be a king or queen for a day!

Let's speak French!

NUMBERS

1 un
2 deux
3 trois
4 quatre
5 cinq
6 six
7 sept
8 huit
9 neuf
10 dix

Bonjour
Hello

S'il vous plaît
Please

Merci
Thank you

*Je voudrais une glace,
 s'il vous plaît.*
I'd like an ice-cream, please.
C'est combien?
How much is it?

Parles-tu anglais?
Do you speak English?

Non
No

Oui
Yes

29

Index